For those almighty alchemists
at Caterpillar Books
~ James Carter

To my parents, Clarice & José
~ Willian Santiago

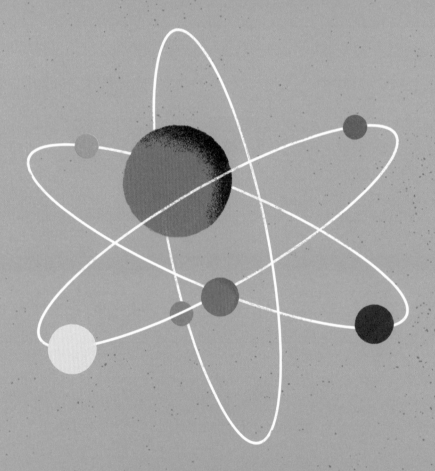

CATERPILLAR BOOKS
An imprint of the LITTLE TIGER GROUP
1 Coda Studios, 189 Munster Road, London SW6 6AW
www.littletiger.co.uk • First published in Great Britain 2020
Text copyright © James Carter 2020
Illustrations copyright © Willian Santiago 2020
A CIP Catalogue record for this book
is available from the British Library
All rights reserved • ISBN: 978-1-84857-983-5
Printed in China • CPB/1800/1367/0120
1 3 5 7 9 10 8 6 4 2

Once Upon an Atom

Questions of Science

James Carter
Illustrated by Willian Santiago

LITTLE TIGER

LONDON

From **BIG** things
to **little** things
invisible to
living things.

From cool things
to hot things
there's nothing
that it's not things.

It's **SCIENCE**
and it's many things
actually it's

EVERY

THING!

From **BIG BANGS**

SCIENCE

It begins in

to **tiny** atoms

tells us why things happen.

as *curious minds*

QUESTIONS of so many kinds.

WHY do leaves turn red and gold?

WHY do fireworks explode?

WHAT are

whizzes

bangs

expansions?

They're all

CHEMICAL REACTIONS!

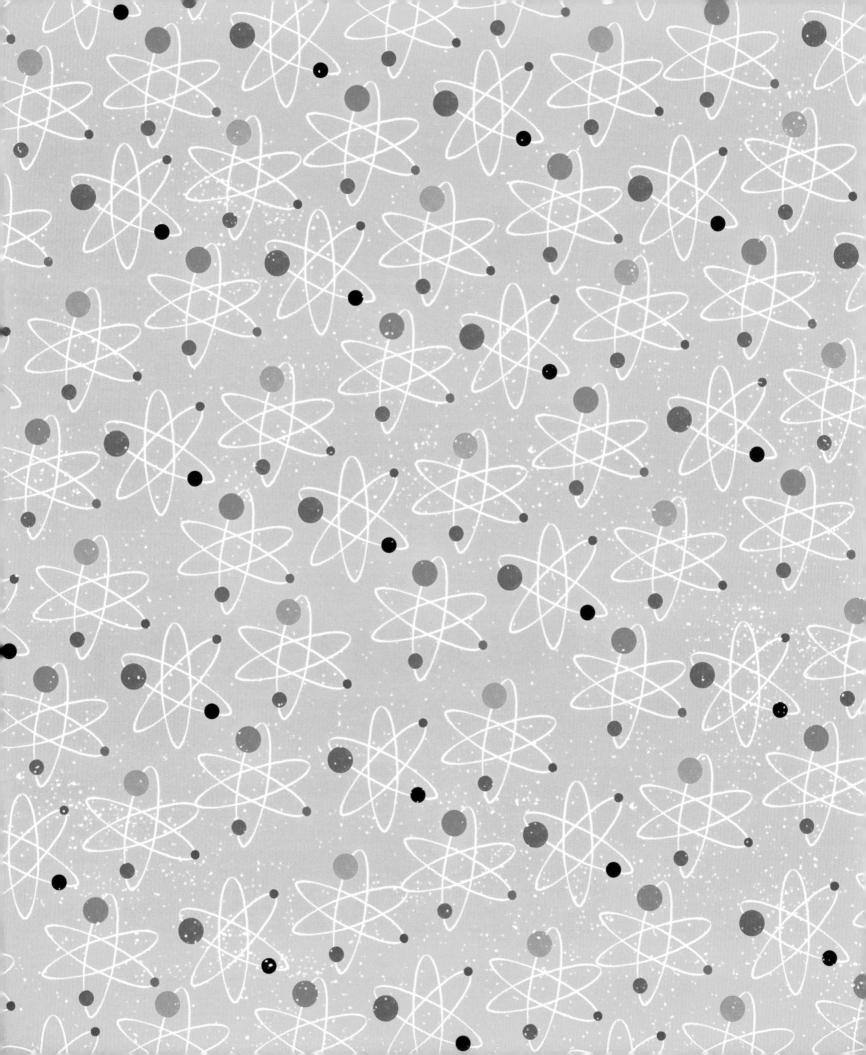

WHAT makes everything you see?

It's all **atoms** basically

the **smallest** particles can be.

This **SCIENCE** is called

CHEMISTRY!

What powers our **machinery** **inventions** and **technology?**

Our **factories** and **industry?**

The answer's

ELECT

RICITY

WHAT can't be seen and has no sound?

Makes **feathers** fall from **sky** to **ground?**

Keeps **boats** afloat upon the **sea?**

That

mighty

force

called

GRAVITY

We live in one great universe and **PHYSICS** tells us how that works.

So how did life appear and why?

then **sky?**

then **land**

In **oceans** first

It's **EVOLUTION**

that's the thing

how life grew

FINS

grew **WINGS.**

grew **LIMBS**

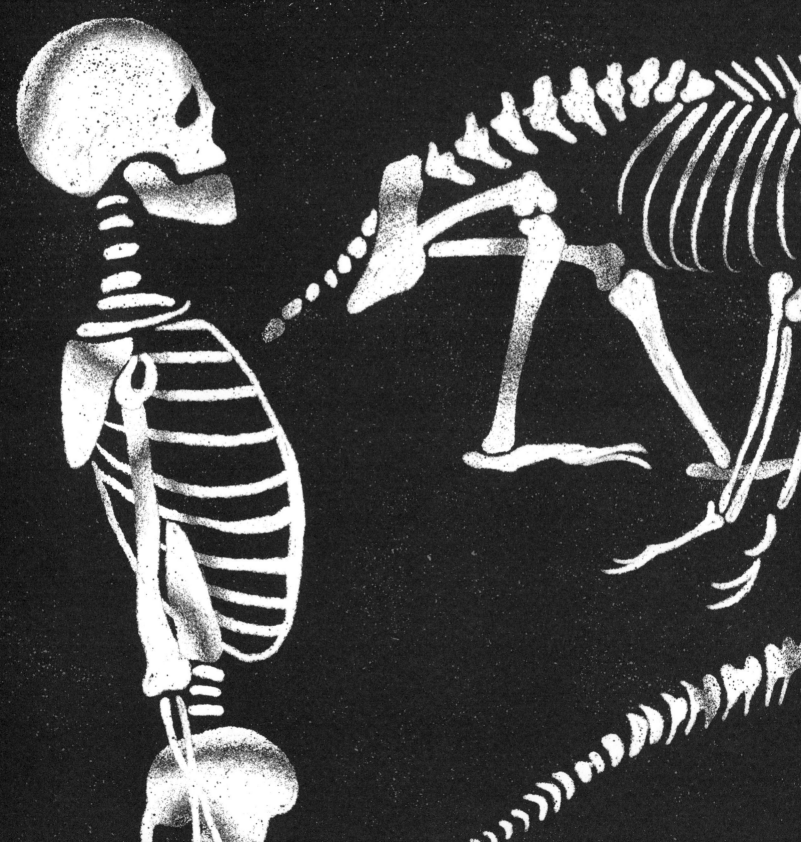

see skeletons
and muscles, guts

lungs and livers
brains and blood!

From **tiny** flowers
to **TOWERING** trees

life blooms in great diversity

that science is **BIOLOGY.**

WHAT do all those SCIENTISTS do?
They try to see the world anew.

From out in space, beneath the seas
in deserts or laboratories.

They try things out, **experiment**
they draw, they build, what's more – **INVENT.**

Now **WHO** knows what the **FUTURE** is?

Find out...

become a
SCIENTIST!

It's all a question of

S cience is one of those things you can be doing without even realising it. Breathing, blowing up a balloon, kicking or catching a ball. They all happen because of science.

C ould you jump up and touch a cloud? Why not? *Gravity*. It's that invisible but powerful force that holds everyone and everything together – from down here on Earth to way across the expanding universe.

I magine there are three doors. Each opens into its own exciting world of science: on one it says 'Physics', another 'Chemistry' and the other 'Biology'. One day you will peer behind these three doors at school, or maybe as your job!

E arly microscopes were invented in Greece in 100CE; the Ancient Egyptians invented the lighthouse in 280BCE; the Chinese came up with compasses and lenses for glasses a thousand years ago. Key scientific discoveries have been made throughout history!

N ebulae and nuclei, quarks and quasars, photons and protons – these are just some of the wonderful words invented by science. Whenever something is discovered or invented it needs to be given a brand new name!

C urie was a scientist who developed X-ray machines, Einstein and Hawking changed the way we think about the universe, Darwin told the world about evolution and Anning was a pioneering fossil hunter. Scientists like these help us in so many important ways.

E ver thought of being a scientist yourself? What would you like to discover? A new star? A cure for a disease? Or maybe you could invent a robot to tidy your bedroom?